In the Gorge

Poems

Brandon Krieg

Codhill Press
New Paltz, New York

CODHILL

Codhill books are published by David Appelbaum for Codhill Press
 First Edition

Cover and book design by Alicia Fox

Library of Congress Cataloging-in-Publication Data

Names: Krieg, Brandon, author.
Title: In the gorge: poems / Brandon Krieg.
Description: First edition. | New Paltz, New York : Codhill Press, [2017]
Identifiers: LCCN 2017015870 | ISBN 1930337930 (acid-free paper)
Classification: LCC PS3611.R53 A6 2017 | DDC 811/.6—dc23
LC record available at https://lccn.loc.gov/2017015870

for Ezra

CONTENTS

THREE

In the Gorge

ONE

Dominion

I found this shattered
badger, tent stake nailing it
through the eye to earth.

Into the tall grass I hurried,
wearing its crown of flies.

On the Missouri after Election Day

Rock ring in the road, red-black coals
abandoned by hunters, smoldering in rain.
Empty stand at forest's edge, tree house
where silent grown men sat imagining
the thickly-veined necks crowned
with counted points in their crosshairs crumpling.

The billionaire gloating at the podium
spoke straight from his headache to them.
They must have swaggered
into the city, rifles casually swinging,
working themselves up to maybe
burn down the big library, with its
"to be a co-worker in the kingdom of culture,"
its "We shall overcome."

I walk on alone, climb a bank
by the river uniform as though
a bulldozer pushed it there. Beyond it,
on packed sand, a stack of washed-up
logs too damp to make a pyre of
to send these snagged sandals, cooler tops, and tires
as distress signal up to the empty sky.

My thoughts rise instead, drift
a thousand miles upstream, where men
who looked like me stood smugly on a hill
of bison skulls, posing, having cleared the way
for my great-grandfather to grab a ranch,
build a house in town modeled after his fraternity
he could line his Harvard Classics up in and be
righteous and white.

At my feet, a sycamore leaf larger than my face
I could bury my face in and weep,
hoping someone on the far bank
might see me kneeling here and say,
"He is not one of the worst, he just lets the worst
make it easy for him, and is ashamed."

I put on the sycamore mask. In this bizarre play,
owl tufts flicked up, I dance this owl dance.
Not of soundlessly plummeting night
for the small pulse, but of lamely hopping,
car-broken in the cage of some nature museum,
symbol of this very human compassion.

I rage against it a little, then eat from its open hand.

Last Plague

The prophets are done foretelling.
They sit two to a suitcase,
too languid to brush away flies.
Whether they told truths or lies
they are going where they are going.

The sure sound
of an acorn striking ground,
that's surely something!
The prophets aren't listening.
They are sick of the teeth in their mouth.
They are going to meet a king
who is vegetable, mineral, or nothing.

The sea is still bigger than an oat.
A slope is no place for a table.
The prophets are neither
prescient nor culpable,
only languid and heard.
They have never been so heard.
There is a word for what they are feeling:
ahistorical.

Everything's already occurred
to them, the prophets.
They disregard the cicadas'
sudden aural shimmering
in an oak, the infant's
untaught gazing upward.

Lapse in Autumn

Find a bare oak branch to walk with like returning
a lopped limb to the painful place,

follow a jagged dry
side creek, rubble heap
of broken amphorae
                                        into which
lost gods sorted seeds.

A vault in Norway
stores every kind of Earth-seed now
in three-ply foil packages
for mice teeth after us—

so many forms for
passing milk
into the years' revolving mouths,

for the forest to walk through the forest.

Acorn and Bead

Three goslings in green fluff shivering,
the tree frog's bubbled delicate inhaling, the muskrat
pushing up pond's skin with its dark lamp

remind me of you asleep in your crib.
I regret pedaling through a cloud of gnats
because you cried out

when a falling acorn struck your hand.
You wake, bald and pudgy,
a tiny old man.

I remember the "shut-ins"
with their tubes and hanging faces
the church group brought meals to.

I want to be there to bring meals to old you.
You laugh. I laugh,

sliding like a dew bead on a strand of web
far past my own death.

Water Music

A mother thumps
her infant's back:
pleasure of a drum.

Little milk-breath,
and, because clouds
filled her breasts,

little cloud-unclouding
breath. Even loftiest
thought of water is

water escaping
through a watery net
suffering presses

lip to nipple,
eye to clouding
eye to the frets.

The Monitor

I hear the waves slapping higher
on the planks. Are you awake?
I hear a fire leaning on the door.
Someone should check on him.
He's only turning in his sleep.
But listen. Lightning bugs
are sizzling out in a vast
sealed vault. Claws of canned laughter
are scratching inside the wall.
Something soft and heavy
is thudding in a dryer, and wire
from a hacked battery
is being stripped by tiny hands.
He's turning. And you are
not out of your dream. And I—
just now I thought that pillow
squeezed between your knees
was his head. Sleep.
I can't. Nobody came for me
in that district of dark mortgages
where the people wore the masks
of dried tears, having crushed
the things they imagined
their hands were protecting.
I know. Sometimes I seem to hear
my own dead father's voice calling
into a speaker he's far away from,
saying he is coming for me now,
just as fast as the Earth is turning.

The Great Offscreen

Detroit

Loitering on Earth,
they shared a light,
and did the Too-stressed,
and did the Blind-sight,
between steel buoys
laid down in rows
on the jagged revetment
where the river slows.

Raising Styrofoam grails
of cold shrimp dal
and fifths of Old Crow,
they did the Great Offscreen,
beating hollow metal
at another country
(one equally vying
to empty its meters,
archive its soul).

They did the Prosthetic Pregnancy
(left by the studio),
passing it, wearing it,
feeling it kick.
In burning-roof dusk,
they fell on the buoys,
and beat on the buoys,
and clung to the buoys,
shouting *My Child! My Child!*

On the radio I heard this storm

that blurried between sweeps
of wiper blades the rolling rural world
and backlit suddenly a door-less
one-room schoolhouse blocked in with bales of hay
was traveling my direction at my speed.

I turned the knob to raise the human voices
above the drilling droplets as one man
who died at 89 today (and was being honored) confessed
to an interviewer years ago the difficulty of giving up
French horn to compose orchestral works.
I thought I must be passing countless forks

and intersections obscured
by this semi I closely followed,
each leading to some hard-won
hallowed-to-someone ground,

then my attention came to rest again
on the reaching-me-clearly breaking
voice of a woman testifying

she thought fireworks
were going off in a theater,
reached to find her daughter's
arm limp, was pinned

on top of her by a bullet in her own spine.
The wipers shrieked

suddenly in no rain, and I saw that storm she and I
were caught in traveling

every direction at every speed.

Dusk Fugue

looking down from an overpass
looking up through the canopy
the contrails the sunset
are not different things

the mine and the prison
in the hairs on our heads

your face in my hands,
I see where a canyon
goes too steep for grass

last colors before stars
under the skins of the apples
(dropped in piles for flies)
last colors before stars
in the flies' shimmering bodies

in our bodies bright salmon
stand beneath sunflowers
from our mouths an oak's breath
talks justice at a benefit

the stripped terraces of a mine
mean your voice in my hand
the barred terraces of a prison
mean olives and wine

coordinated sprinklers
keep the coal mounds wet
a phone vibrates a nerve
agent twitches to death
the boy in his father's arms

some will be shielded
by the wave as it passes
somehow my face
is not even wet
my mouth opened and said

mine and prison
apple and fly
sunflowers coal mounds
his boy and mine
the wave and your face
the deaths and the benefits
are not different things

last colors before
the canyon goes
too steep for grass

Temporary Dwelling

Valley either side,
I on the spine, this way

goldenrod, this
chaparral. Far down,

still roans, a rubbled
ledge, one

cloud-eclipsed then
brilliant house

from which someone
would see me as

gold blazonry (a live-
oak's leaves,

a pine's pitched
cones, a roughened

sandstone firebreak
road's ascent to

sun) a cloud-bank
shadow crosses gone.

Verges

On these sands sorrow
is alien, small, dispersible

all ways as ants
from a gull's skull.

Joy, too, is introduced,

not indigenous, wracked
wig of stems and roots

exposed, with closed inflorescent
eyes. Unison, unison,

dead cry, silenter than sand.

No—to the grass—I say
no—my one sound—

that flashes ten thousand *nows*.

*

In the great grass river,
wind shows silvers,
I wade in.

On the edge in flickers
you are there and
not there, your shining hair

lifts or is lost
in the seething seaming;
one way the river

is green and you;
the other way you
and silver. I can't say you are
with me, you are
more than with.

*

Scale by scale,
sand climbs
the acorn cap.

We won't be buried into vaster
scales, I think, and so
hold the nut until an empty tone

from deepest generation
reaches me,

drop it in my windy
bootprint, go

whistling from every edge of me.

*

Wind's sway finds shape
in dunegrass tips.
Thick stalks,

a scatter-plot of
deer pellets. From any
available source, the stalks

take. The wind
through me reveals the intricate
quicksilvers of the short-lived.

*

Eddy in the great
grass river.

Faces flicker,
overlay: you

in a mask of years,
green   silver.

Wind shivers, the mask
falls, you are
there   gone.

*

Nature—I leave it in vaults
of the Late

Standardized, in lovely
19c. books, so others may
achieve by its dismissal

the righteous un-naïve. I walk
sands beneath branching
craze-shapes
like cracks
in the
glaze
of this
brittle blue skybowl lately

unearthed, enduring

in despite of trash, jetwash,
endless highwayside.

I walk in deepest despite.

*

Old symmetry,
easy beauty, let me be.

I also want to know
the drift of speckled weeds

before that widest symmetry.

*

Sassafras sails one
yellow leaf down
the dune's steeps.

It lands on the surface
of the great

grass river—lamp
of contrast,
shy of
symmetry, shining of

its own particularity—
light by which
to find the way back

to this day among days.

*

Haughty ambient
Alhambras malignant
with buttresses, building up

over the sand-road, unaware
of tremulous reflections
where waves vie, the cumulous palaces

glide ahistorical, as if over
the long corridor before birth.

*

Thank brevity gulls race
their shadows over
sand—goodbye—thank brevity

the sole's imprint is blown out
of each footprint and in one

shallow depression
a dried white moth's papery flickers
remind me—thank

brevity for all other than
you: whose day in me is

sand over
sand without
end, whose hours

have broken their glass.

*

Take affirmation, more
difficult than indifference—take it.

Wind-pressed grass tips scratch
worm-tracks in sand windy sand

erases. Pull a tip and follow
the livid arcs it traces.

*

Cumulous palaces
gate the far waters:
pink gold and unison.

I speak into this silvergreen blade
three distinctions

you you you

and float it out—news
of the great grass river.

As Continents Slid

I woke in
cricket dark. He nursed
between us. I'd dreamt,
hanging from eras
over eras, a reservoir
blinked out, savannahs swept
through stanchions
and dry canals,
a quarry was filled and
forested and drowned
at the fault as
continents slid.

I smelled his hair,
kissed his neck.
Yesterday I gave him
a heavy-headed grass stem
pulled from the side
of the tire-rutted mud.
He tripped, dropped
the sunlit grass in grass,
stood and carefully
picked it up again,
acolyte of one afternoon.

TWO

The Removes

Lost you where poppies climbed from fields
between houses, where screens on the back of bus seats
showed the living in the now of an obsolescent ship, where a mandala
and a barcode shared the last wall before the sun set

between houses,   screens
   flashing already like disconnected signal fires:
                                        the last wall before
your askance was overwritten

by flashing   disconnected.

*

Terraces of semblance

then: roofs like a ruined organ,
sky a wide sustain.

Terraces of
summer, dials

turned to alpenlight.
A wide sustain

dials
even us.

Turned to alpenlight:
that you

fathoms and pervades as

day.
Then
fathoms
opens.

*

I, alone, across
the shadow of a fountain falling back curved,
a moment returning vaster
than itself.

Shadows of curved
time, the blue in a sepia eye,
the impossibility
we met before

time—the blue in
an arch's sky-through our sign
we have before
in secret. In truth, anything—

an arch's sky-through—
is only solitude too diminished to lie
in secret in. Truth, anything
I could call you

is diminished. To lie
a moment vaster
I call
alone *across*.

*

A worn-down sandstone cliff on the coast,
the path to it crumbled to nothing,
could it have been you and I
there once if there is no trace of it left?

The path
into the applause I thought I heard far off,
          there is no trace of it:
waves carve the accidental cubism of the cliffs.

The accident   of
our incidence:
          from every angle
the vanishing point passes through the glance.

*

If it could be as never
before, then you. No,
if it could be as always more
piercingly, then through

                    you no
word would intervene.
If it could be as always
but with cloudshadow on the dial and no

word
for it in me, then you, and magnified.
But with   no
lake seen through to an altar wrecked

    in me,   magnified
is only a mountain assuming its reflection in a
lake seen
as the picture of itself.

  Only a mountain
piercing   through
the picture of itself
   could be as you.

*

I say you and no one knows what it means.
In the moraine's shadow, I might trace
the vein in your groin as sun touches a stream.

When your hair. When your cusps.
But it is afterward already.

The you of you eludes
even the particular futility of my joy.

I have pebbled an altar to all
aches, and cattails point.
A thousand perhaps directions.

Walls, a wedged bridge, horses browse,
all contingencies parallel except
the vein in your groin as sun touches a stream.

Aches and cattails point.
I have pebbled an altar to all
the you of you eludes—

bald cairn, poor form. Waves anonymize
even the particular futility of my joy.

When your hair. When your cusps.

A thousand perhaps directions
in the moraine's shadow, I might trace,
absolved to tributary.

But it is afterward already.

*

We looked down
on the river from a high window:
nothing else was there in the canyon
where   the sun was always about to set.

On the river
we could see the jade-colored pebbles
wherever the sun was
as if there were no water at all.

We could see
no reflection,
as if there were no water at all,
though the sound was unmistakable:

no   projection of ourselves,
an alien resonance, yet
                                        unmistakable
as that you and I were there—

a   resonance
I had not known I had always known, like
   that you   I
saw then as myself. I knelt then in the grief

I had not known I had always known.
Nothing else was there in the canyon.

More Soon

marked the mine
1912.

A hundred years later,
found a buck there,

rack hooked
in a wire fence,

shook free,
scaled the canyon.

Lapse in Spring

Crossed dewgrass hillocks
    of the abandoned gravel mine,
wild onion
    on my breath. Picked up white stones
from where ten thousand years ago
glaciers set them down and fled.
    Hands froze.
    Her breasts
under wool, the fine down
on our toddler's rounded shoulders!
    Drove.
On the outskirts, towering
beeches had pushed up through
the glass roofs of the greenhouses.

In the Gorge

At dusk, drove down from the pass, and, cool through the vents,
this smell:

onion fields,
diesel barges,

where the Bridge of the Gods fell epochs ago, its absence in the glass

of the industrial
waters reflected:

windshields glaring on an arc between two identical states.

I stopped then:
sundown dimensioning

steep basalt walls, onion trucks, tracks of topped stalks, crying without feeling.

Notes from the Anthropocene

Dust of trains settles on the vineyard.
My hands aren't even good for your body.
The mountains have been miniaturized.
We can't seem to make ourselves vulnerable.
Has the Earth been raised or lowered
to become this echo chamber
of domes broadcast on the river?
Olives beneath the stone wall
appear later, pitted, in bowls.
Nothing is required of us.
I'd like to feel genuinely small.
Seed tufts catch on barbed wire.
Gilt scales seal the eyes of the figure.
Fleets sail into future languages.
Our love is too translatable.
Your hands aren't even good for my body.
The gods must have been laughing
to see us touch spicy mouths to genitals,
the hunger not put out.
Or worse, no one was watching.
Confetti speckles the river
falling from who knows where.
The song wheel keeps on spinning
though the singer has long been dead.
Has the earth been raised or lowered
that projectors stream over its faces?
From a hill of ancient grave mounds
we watch the coal plant's candy-striped smokestack
vent strata of Earth into sky.
If we could only reside in the sky.
Whatever we do to the Earth
the sky becomes more beautiful.

Throughscape

Chicago-bound
train—horses, heads down
shake snowy manes

at orchard-edge—slashed
cornstalks radiate
over-hill like hackles
of a bent feather—gaze a little higher sky is not

bi- or trisected by power
lines—snow drifts diagonally against
the stanchions of the empty

band shell—above us suddenly a smooth-upthrust
landfill-hill—a swan ducks under
a pond's ice-edge—*Rent the Rain*

on a silo outside a mill—bootprints
from base to base
around a snowy infield—cattails
in the low places—seeps in
reeds—yellowish

hanging willow threads yellowing
a flowing ditch—green rectangle of ice
on the treatment pond—yachts cinched
in white plastic shrink-wrap—a hundred

blue pallets stacked—black
sandbags—mounds of pushed
snow in a lot—frozen lake waves
under smokestacks—snow on fertilizer

sacks—two men
walk out of the Whistle Stop Bar at 10 a.m.,
shield their eyes—

behind me: "I don't like the fact that D is living
with her, it's like they're
planning something"—a patch of forest cut into
evenly-spaced log-pyramids—a horse head

insignia on three cars of a passing freighter
we stop for—geese trace
the river between outbuildings—
we tunnel again through the predicted

snow—new snow

clings to the north side
of every oak—enormous sheds
loom—*Gary Works*—broken cross
of a telephone pole

snapped into a ditch—tall
grass, *United States Steel*—

black slag foothills carved
into model floodplains—snow-dust showing sinuous
cracks in the wide empty

Horseshoe Casino lot—tiny sparks
in a cavernous hangar—snow on the black
coal-heaps in a hundred railcars—power

lines disappearing
into the far falling white—a glimpse

of the gray lake between
factory and factory—“world’s
busiest freight corridor”
the conductor says in the crackling

speaker—houses hunker
in refinery fumes—leafless
vines nerve a mile of barbed wire—

No Wake Area
above the harbor.

Inherit the Earth

Three snowy days and this town is rich in icicles.
If you couldn't care you were never a kid.
How do you prefer your glint and glare?
Second-hand, pan to the candidate's daughter's
pearl-harnessed neck, the glancing opaque
watch face of the candidate's son?
My father grabbed one shimmering
ice-pike down from the eaves for me
like he'd stolen lightning from the sky.
You'd never know, to see it now,
that disintegrating tract house there—
under the refinery's flame, beside the quarry—
was once the middle of everywhere.

Winter Night

Still wind chime,
icicles, I look through
to the forest strangeness:
this smooth white fern-less
understory under
new snow. I have an idea
of an owl's idea of silence:
vast as a moraine shelf
recalls its retreated
glacier down its entire
striated length. That vastness—
I'd have it too, I thought,
if I lost you. I have too often
agreed with myself.

Anti-Narcissus

I can't be fast as the filmed snake whiplashes.
I can't be fast as the heron snaps.
I can be slow.

The child streaked from crying against its mother in the bus shelter
clutches the plastic chess piece
picked from the complex's dumpster.

Under a stoplight at night, someone's son's pimpled face
glares red. It is so quiet,
a little down from here the roads may no longer intersect.
The sumac lamps

have flaked flameless.
In the import store I lifted a plastic sack
of red powder from Turkey, turned it hourglass-over,
put it back

still as the handful-sized heap of maple seeds
nestled by the engine block
all winter is now,

scooped out and scattered on the snow-crust
like chips of moon in
Antarctic ice.

Each moon-chip is a seed. No human will live
to see it flower. There is something in me so slow
it will be around even then.

But to know what that is
would be like seeing in this bucket's disk of frosted ice
my reflection.

Mirror to Mirror

"My face in thine eye, thine in mine appears. . ."

—John Donne

Of that declension through self-similars I'm thinking: galaxies
spiraling in the whorls

of her fingers, lighting the very nerves of me; she
quakes; I

likewise in her eyes ache to release lightning,
floodplain, veins

of a leaf—anything wildly branching—
the deciduous

consciousness of our archaic
kind. Oh germ

of mind cast in nautilus
dark, take—

in this dimension a
mirror

held up to a
mirror

mak
es.

Evening Bell

Refugee of two gods, three wars,
five cities, and that glancing touch

on your face is what made you
look finally up: a man leaning
over the bar of a black fire-

escape, unsteadily
clipping his dun-colored hair down,
stood you in your pulse

like a belled ungulate
tangled in a wire fence,

hearing its own ringing
as the stars would hear it.

Temple Builders' Lament

Swallows string cat's cradles
above the roofs.
A robed young woman
locked out into the morning
smiles, as if tricked,
at the sky. Later her face
appears in every window
of a passing train, like a CD skipping.
After-dinner rain
empties the hot streets, a fly
draws a rectangle endlessly
in the center of the room.
In that frame: the sculptor's
journal-notes for the lost
lecture: "Building the Temple
of the Future Within Us."
He guessed we'd find ourselves
in frames within frames, but
couldn't have imagined these same
acts of resistance the only left us:
watching bats and butterflies flicker
over the canal; picking apricots
on a slope nearly too steep
to stand on; opening
an old book, again and again.

Late August Aubade

Bushwick

Rain through a wire window screen,
our only relief. Be endless
gray to us, do not be brief.

A neighbor has hung her clothes to soak.
Bring her household endless luck.
Find out the roots of her withered beets.
Find out the roots of her withered belief
in anything—anything.
Do not be brief.

Commence the new wet century, please
not the working week.

A siren calls through the rain—
make way for this pain.
Saturday's sambas are done,
the back yards are strung
with bulbs, but empty.
Under the umbrella is no card game.

Let us linger, my love and me,
beside this window, let us confess to this
unlikely beautiful
wire-crossed weedy grotto
we have never gone willingly
to doldrum offices.

Pour streams down these panes
to shadow-pattern our nakedness.

Give us lightning, clutch us
in good fearfulness.

Give us thunder, shake free
the clinging seeds.

Then let delicious drops diminuendo endlessly.

THREE

On Not Reaching the Summit

Up there
pixels freeze
cloud-flow
hawk-float
grass-seethe

into a viewpoint
equidistant from every point
on the terabyte grid.
I lie down

beside the last elm
where the path begins to switchback
up a steep headland of
grass grass

and raisin by raisin
eat a handful of raisins
in glad unsuccess
and countless winds

bending one lupine bell tower
so the shadow of its blackhalo
of bees intermittently
blackhaloes me,

smug as a minor Byzantine
in my niche filigreed
with catchfly, paintbrush, and fescue.

Hammer Sect

All morning cutting
steps in steep summer
snow lanes, wading
graysilt glacial
gorge-cutter waters
that ring the nerve

from ankle to roots
of teeth, we of the same
hammer, brother,
driven *in in*,
pried out again
in bald day—
peregrine shadows

passing over us—
we who slept on the rim
of stars creeping over ice
now labor over
thousands of fire-polished
trunks snapped across
the trail hard to trace—

"If you come to a Y
you have gone too far."

We have come to
many Ys and now to this
lightning-made
colonnade of
scorch-white branchless Ionics
circling a green floor
patterned with grasses, mosses,
avalanche lilies, enter

this altar of the rhyme
of banded fallen feather, lines
scored by fallen boulders
on the face of the highest

fields of ice, enter this
towering absence
of any tradition
through which to make sense of it.

Kings Mountain

Hottest July in memory. Salmonberries already
sweet along the trail. The steeps
where only helicopters could plant fir seeds
after fiery decades
                                        are again in entire shade.

I scratch in a spiral notebook
rolled into PVC pipe at 3000 feet my name
above me always now.
Remembering this will not help me live in a far plains city,
I think.
                    Below,
in a rectangular clear-cut, firs at random left standing
cast shadows at exactly the same angle,
analog clock hands synchronized by
some unseen hand, the same

                    converting algae into diesel fuel,
                    augmenting athletes
                    with myoglobin of whales,
                    altering the mixture
                    of three rivers behind a dam,
                    printing an implant
                    to hold open an infant's esophagus,
                    transforming brains
                    into lossless interfaces. . .

At the highway again, out of water,
I find the trail to the Wilson
behind a windowless van
flanked on either side by prisoners
pushing through tall grass
bear-like picking berries
the hazard orange of their vests.

They stand at once above the grass
to stare at me in my otherworld
where whatever watches over me
lets me pump water from the river whenever I please.

Fireweed

North of Timber Management Solutions,
amid the gaping

concentric sun-circuitry of truncated fir stumps,
fireweed flourishes,

fireweed crackles like the feedback of a sun-struck
accord.

Fireweed, fireweed, uninvited honeyed
weather where mere acres were,

radio telescopes sound space for life, satellites snail
the fishbowl night

surveilling some world. Your availing escapes
undigitized, your all-

resuming conflagration even gone dark holds
this hillside up against the night sky.

What Good

I'm in a bowing mood.
I walk along a wood
colored like a cliff of various
stones in various lights,
sandstone, hematite,

flaking away in wind.
Tulip poplar leaf, flake
of yellow-finding-out-
four-pointedness,
what good is bowing

to so little of all?
The fine point
of a woodpecker's bill
rings a tall maple
like a dense bell.

The Oak-Whale

Oak,
sun-lung,
holds its full
inhale longer
than the long inhale
of the blue whale.

I live along the bottom,
never needing
to breach, permeable

to light across
this blood-oak barrier.

Dogged Today

I plop down on the rocky prow of this
American coast careering toward sunset,
thinking of those dogged men

of the North Sea, who lowered their nets
over the sunken
Dogger Bank—ten-thousand-years lost

island—and pulled them up fouled
with colossal mammal bones and crude
stone implements—clues,

perhaps, to raise very Atlantis
into light; curiosities at least
to fill some museum's queues.

They pocketed a few trinkets, heaped
the mass of artifacts in the aft,
motored over a steep undersea cliff, and
dropped them back into the deep.

They were fishermen.
They wanted to lift cod in their nets, not
the bones again.

I am away from the world, sick
of its anecdotes. I've come to drop
these men, their bones, the whole

pantheon of petrified gods,
to lift anything—the very shit-streaked,
fish-reeking stones—

into the light of this day.

Barking at the Tide

My father cracks the sex
off twenty cooked male crabs,
snaps free steaming headpieces,
strips the gills, and hoses
the green life-stuff into grass.

He leans heavy on me as a sack of salt
to stand, hairline fracture in his knee
barking pain. A half-emptied sack of salt
sags by the kettle—by some cosmic irony
it makes the meat cook sweet.
If Anchises had been twice
Aeneas's weight, I wonder,
would they have escaped together as ash?

He limps away. I press the purple throb
where earlier his new dog
bit the back of my right hand.
I had reached for his slimy ball, his little all
he would crash into the wave-wall
to retrieve. He is life unconscious
of limitation, in slippery pulsing skin.

Tonight I pick a shelled crab, skinny as an eel,
that taints my tongue with iodine.
By the beach bonfire no amount of wine
can flush the taste, or keep my father's voice
from going dry. *It should have been a radio voice,*
he says, *not a salesman's.*
He knows I'm the only audience
wired to receive this signal
past its end, and troubles himself
to be voluble.

Tonight's broadcast reaches
over an antipodal sea my own wine darkness:
his infant grandfather in Kohlberg given
with an enlarged heart to "gypsies,"
returned two weeks later to survive.
Apocryphal man!
The father-fire belches sparks
up to the stars. The stars remain.

The next morning in brace
he walks his black Cerberus up over Fishing Rock
to bark at the tide in the shining mussel beds.
He goes before I wake, to escape,
perhaps, what he thinks I might have said.
I never can get it right, whatever it would be:
that I'm not ready to learn by cosmic irony
what his fall would add to the sea
in terms of salt. That I'm not ready
to know what beyond words it would take from me.

Squawfish

Vulgar name for the Northern pikeminnow

It was my luck: the three-dollar bounty
on the squawfish that year, that preys
on salmon smolts and has the fine bones woven
tightly into flesh—sure mark of a trash fish.

It has a puckered suckermouth, slimy spade-shaped
scales, and a bald gold eye that begs you to smash it.
I would not even remove a small one from my line
but would swing it from the water

like a lantern on a chain, dashing its light out
on the rocks, sometimes finding gold pieces
of eye on the rocks the next day.
It inspired cruelty in me I explained

to my younger brother was mercy—"Put them out
of their dumb misery." He came to love those
times when mercy was required of him, acting
like a rush of water that cannot help itself

when the new channel is cut. The summer before he left
for the war we fished every evening and caught
ten-thousand-dollars worth between us and bought
a drift boat to take down the Rogue in spring.

I haven't made a cast since he died. The boat is adrift
on the side of my house and sometimes fills with rain.
I go to sit where we fished to be sure he is not
casting in the eyes that cover the rocks in my dream.

Delineations

town's end
fenced lot
no gate

riprap
seawall
shell yard

snapped clam
blue egg
three halves

green glass
high grass
old sign

you could
live here:
outline

Biking to Haven

South Haven, Michigan

"... in an era when water might replace oil as the most
contested commodity."

—*New York Times*, Aug. 25, 2015

The 37-mile paved-over former
railroad right of way crossed, I dismount, and
in tired leisure eat

the packed sandwich by the lake, remembering
her up to the wrist in sticky dough laughing, blowing

hair out of her eyes, asking me to scatter
cool white fine-ground handfuls from the sack
onto the board where she was kneading,

handfuls from who knows where—China likely
as Nebraska, cheap
as manna, as

incredible. I lean against this
lighthouse at the end of the pier, its history
over: a symbol to point a camera at,
like a dead derrick or abandoned
factory graffito. My image, too,

has traveled, just now, to the ends of Earth
through a Polish couple's phone—I am backdrop
to their embrace like this charter boat returning
to the mouth of the Black River,
a child in camouflage onboard
holding up a bright Chinook

like my child-self crossing after fearful hours
the treacherous Columbia bar
in a boat steered by my father.

I am brief haven of father and son returning
to that now imaginary
port, shimmering against this wide,

placid source of future wars.

Receiver

A condemned house's catalpa
floats orchid-like
white flowers into the road.

On tires pumped with exhalations
borrowed from mussel, chipmunk, bison, brewery, man
lying under a bench wiping his dog's eye with a napkin,
I receive joy prepared for me

forty years ago in France
by workers soldering fast
this ten-speed's diamond frame, listening
to a forgotten match
on a radio now buried beneath a layer of weeds.

No, no
signal longer reaches there.
Yet some resonance rouses me to stand
on pedals, reach into this sun-filled cloud
of downy seeds blowing from the wood beside the creek,
feel the leafy shade cherished by some future traveler
tick my hand.

Receiver (II)

My bike's tires crush
fallen berries
with a pleasing popping sound.

A flock lifts up,
a flock I'm in,
                    veers at once
into an oak and I go on.

The signals I've missed, so many, and yet,

smoke rises
from each of the ten greenhouses in the row,
ice sheets slip
into the creek between substation and auto body
showing opal pebbles,
a shaking woman pours out
a vial of sand into a yard,
a single day

removes its disguise of obviousness.

                                        Many days.
                                        Many disguises.

Beyond the Useful Life

A crow drinks rain from a paint bucket's overturned lid.

Two teens lie on a rock after swimming, waiting for their cut-off fatigues to dry.

Steelhead suspend inside the cab of a sunken Ford where the river bends.

A heap of sun-bleached shells shines beside the oysterhouse.

Under three bales of rusted fencing, a garter snake rests.

The barn's last remaining pane flashes as I bike past.

ACKNOWLEDGMENTS

Berkeley Poetry Review: "Throughscape"
Blue Mesa Review: "Temporary Dwelling"
Cincinnati Review: "Lapse in Spring," "On Not Reaching the Summit"
Commonweal: "Anti-Narcissus," "On the radio I heard this storm"
Conjunctions: "The Removes"
DIAGRAM: "Verges"
FIELD: "Beyond the Useful Life"
Harpur Palate: "Biking to Haven," "Dusk Fugue," "Hammer Sect," "Kings Mountain"
Heron Tree: "Temple Builders' Lament"
Inscape Literary Magazine: "Late August Aubade"
Iron Horse Literary Review: "Barking at the Tide," "Dogged Today"
The Journal: "Winter Night"
Minnetonka Review: "Squawfish"
North American Review: "The Oak-Whale"
Owen Wister Review: "Dominion"
Salamander: "Fireweed," "Inherit the Earth," "Mirror to Mirror," "The Monitor"
South Dakota Review: "Acorn and Bead," "Water Music"

ABOUT THE AUTHOR

Brandon Krieg is the author of *Invasives*, a finalist for the 2015 ASLE Book Award in Environmental Creative Writing, and a chapbook, *Source to Mouth.* He grew up in Tualatin, Oregon, and lives in Columbia, Missouri, with his spouse, Colleen O'Brien, and their son, Ezra. He teaches at Westminster College.